Dear Mr. President

Dear Mr. President

Compiled by Stuart Hample

Illustrated by G. Brian Karas

WORKMAN PUBLISHING • NEW YORK

Copyright © 1993 by Naomi-Stuart Productions
Illustrations copyright © G. Brian Karas

Cover and book design by Lisa Hollander

Library of Congress Cataloging-in-Publication Data

Dear Mr. President/compiled by Stuart Hample : illustrated by G. Brian Karas.
p. cm.
ISBN 1-56305-504-X (pbk.)
1. Clinton, Bill, 1946-   —Humor. 2. Clinton, Bill, 1946-   —Correspondence.
3. Children—United States—Correspondence. 4. Children's writings,
American. I. Hample, Stuart E.   II. Karas, G. Brian
E886.2.d.43 1993
973.929'092—dc20   93-14472
CIP

Workman books are available at special discounts when purchased in bulk
for premiums and sales promotions as well as for fund-raising or educational use.
Special editions or book excerpts can also be created to specification.
For details, contact the Special Sales Director at the address below.

Workman Publishing
708 Broadway
New York, NY 10003

Printed in the United States of America

First printing October 1993
10 9 8 7 6 5 4 3 2 1

CONTENTS

Introduction

Inquiries, Warnings & Doubts

Free Advice & F.Y.I.

Requests, Offers & Hopes

Children, as yet untouched by realpolitik and other disillusionments of the adult world, expect their leaders to be perfect. And President Bill Clinton is no exception. True, his high energy, open manner, young daughter and cat are all in his favor. And he's about the same age as their parents, which makes him equally certain to shield them from war, holes in the ozone, poverty, pestilence, racism, and bullies in the school yard. But there's always room for improvement—and children are quick to offer advice.

Their letters, while often humorous and naive, perhaps ought to be taken seriously, for they frequently manage to cut directly to the heart of matters we ostensibly wiser adults find too confusing even to articulate.

And if they reward you with a smile or two, all the better!

Stuart Hample

Inquiries, Warnings & Doubts

Dear President Clinton,

Are you famouser than God?

Annette

Dear Sir
My father said you cut
out star wars. Does that
mean we could not rent it
ever again.

Kevin

Dear Mister Clinton,
If you want to be the President
do you have to have all A's in
school because if you do
then I'm out of luck.

Richard

to mr. president Bill Clinton
how come those guys in the
early times who were presidint
wore those wigs ?
Were they bald or what?

Howard

Dear President Clinton,
What do you think about Hillary to be the President after you? Whould you feel funny to be the first man?

from
Sarah L.M. 4th Grade

Dear Mr. Pres.
Do the secret service guys guard Socks as good as they guard you even though he is just a cat?

Ricardo

Dear President Clinton,

When you are on T.V. you sound like you know every-thing. Do you really or do you just fake it?

Alexandra

Dear Mr. President,

It must be great to be Pres.
and able to call up anybody
you want like Michael Jordan.

From Frederick

Dear Mr. Presidant,

If you and Hillary and Chelsea don't like the food in the White House do you call the F.B.I.?

Katherine

Dear President Clinton,
We saw the Washington Monument.
We saw the Lincoln one and also
the Jefferson one. Will there be one
like them for you or do you
have to wait til you get dead?

Kerry

Dear Mr clinton the persident

On the T.V. show with children you said When you were in school your teacher said you should stop talking so much. I think you better do that now and pay more attention to make jobs for poor people,

Nardi

Dear President Bill Clinton
Are you really good when you play the saxophone or did you pay some guy to hide behind somewhere and play it better so everybody will think it's you.

Josh

Dear President Clinton,

Do you get to own the United States when your the President?

Harvey

Dear Mr Clinton,

When famous people and movie stars come to the White House does Chelsea get to meet them? I think she's verrry lucky to be the president's daughter!

Michelle

Dear Mr. President Bill Clinton,
My mom said your wife is the boss over you. How come? I thought you are supposed to be the most powerful person in the world.

Regis G.

Dear President Mr. Clinton,

Do you go to McDonald's because they give it to you free? Or do you have to pay money like us normal people.

Maura K.

Dear Mr. Clinton,

Do you have to act like a president all the time like when you are eating supper or taking a bath? Or can you be silly sometimes like my father?

Judy

Dear President Clinton,
Do you like pizza?
Is it still hot when
it is delivered to the
White House or do the
guards stop the guy at
the gate and ask questions
so that it always gets cold?

Rachel

Dear President Clinton, Sir,
   Does Chelsea get in
trouble when she forgets to
empty the litter box?
I sure do!

                    Rosa

Dear mister president

I saw your watch you wore on the T.V. show. It looks just like mine which cost $21. I thought if you are the president you are suppose to be rich.

Dennis

Dear President Clinton,

Do those men who guard you all the time even watch you go to the bathroom?

Tim:
Age: 8

Dear Bill Clinton

Do you like Vice President Gore
or do you just hang out with him
because you have to?
Erica

Dear Mr. Clinton,

When you come in to a room and they clap every time, does that mean they really like you or do they just do it because you are the President and they fear your power?

Jo Anne

Dear President Clinton,
You are very nice looking except for the puffy bags under your eyes. You better go to sleep earlier.

Jeanette

Free
Advice
&
F.Y.I.

Dear Pres Clinton
Can you name
all the States?
I can.

Amy

Dear, {President} {Clinton}

Does it bother you that people do cartoons of you? and make you have big cheeks and a weird looking nose and a big belly?

Kitty F.

Dear Pres Clinton,

When you are in church you should pray that you don't goof up so much. Maybe that will help you get it right.

Alfred W.

Dear President Clinton,
why can't Kids vote?
That stinks.

sean

Dear Mr. Clinton—
All of the president's since George
Washington have always been a man.
I don't think that's fair.
                Alexa

Dear Mr. President,
my father says nobody
can please everybody so
you should stop trying
to do it.

Jules

Dear Pres. Clinton,
I think I rather
be a King than the President.
They get to be
King for life but the
President always gets
kicked out.

Joseph

Dear Presidant Clinton,

Do yoy know the Constituion by heart? Then you wouldnt ever have to look up anything and that will give you more time to do your job better.

Ormond

Dear Mr. President Clinton —
My grandmother says she was
out of high school before you
were even born and she would
like to sit you down and give you
a talking to. But don't do it
because she can really be mean.

Dale

Dear President Clinton,

You are very good on television. Maybe when you don't get elected again you could have your own show like Jay Leno.

Martin S.

Dear Presaident Clinton,
If I was the Presaident
and I knew who didn't
Vote for me, I would't do
anything for them.

Charles

Dear Presedent Clinton,

    I think before you and Hillary change everything with the health care you and Her should swap places with two doctors and work in the hospital for one day and see how everything is run.

               Sinserly,
                  Daniel

Dear Mr. President,

You should make some new States, then they would have to do what you want so you can get more laws past.

Lorraine

Dear Mr. President,

To end pollution more People should use bicycles or rollarblades or walk to work and not take cars and buses. First of all it's good for the enviromet. Second of all it's good to lose wait which you could use a lot.

Ralph

Dear President Clintion

You better not brake your promesis or my father will get mad and believe me you do not want that to happen.

Dimitris

Dear President Clinton,
How do you keep track of everyone who works for you? My mother tapes a list on the fridge with your name on it and what your chore is for every day of the week and if you don't do what it says You better watch out!
Cindi

Dear Mr. Clinton,

I wouldn't want to be the President because you have to wear a suit and tie and go to church every Sunday.

Sheldon

Dear Mr. President,

Our social studies teacher said United States government doesn't have enough money to pay the bills so you have to raise taxes. Why don't you just put all that stuff on your credit card like my mom does?

Cheryl

Requests,
Offers
&
Hopes

Dear President clinton,
My teacher read us where
it says in the Declaration
of Indipendence that all
people are created eqal. I
wish you would tell my
brother Joel who always hits
me because I am
smaller so I cant
hit him back

Mark

Bill Clinton!

Sometimes when you have a problem about kids that you can't figure out you should ask Chelsea what she thinks because she is a kid and they know stuff that grown-ups are too stupid to understand.

Walter.

Dear predisent Clinton,
please make lots and
lots and lots and lots
and lots of jobs so my
mother can have
one.

Lawanda

Dear President Clinton

I wish you could make peace in the world.

I wish you could take all the guns out of the store.

I wish you could lower bus fare.

by Yours truly
Kaneaka

Dear Mr. Clinton
Every time I have to sing the Star Spangled Banner I have trouble. Please write a new one that's not so hard.

Victoria

Dear. Mr. Presidant Clinton,
My father made me go to bed before the world series games was over. Please tell him to let me stay up or else make them play Not in the night. His phone number is 546-7803.

Steven R

Dear Mr. Clinton,

I would like to be the president someday but only if you can still have fun.

Fran

Dear President Clinton,
I wish you would tell everyone that white people and black people are the same.

Lila

Dear President,

Please have them pick up the garbage on our street. It smells awful.

Respectfully,
Samuel

Dear President,

Does Chelsea get to wear lipstick? I need to KNOW before Saturday.

Jill

Dear Mr. President,
I want to be the first
President who is a woman
but if I dont get elected
then I will go for movie
star.

Yours very Truly
Lonetta

Dear Bill,
You are a nice President and
I think you are a very good
President (SO far)
Tashika

Dear President Clinton,

Could you please pay teachers more money? I'm sure my teacher (Mrs. Lynn) will like that!

Sincerely,
Julie

Dear President Bill Clinton,
I hope you are not mad
at every Republicin because
my father is one.

Rose Mary G.

Dear President Clinton,

I think it's a good idea to raise the taxes so the goverment will have lots of money but please dont do it to my father because then he will have another phoney excuse to not by me the new nintendo game.

Carrie

Dear President Clinton
Please save the world.

KauoKisha

Dear President Clinton,
I have faith in you.
David

THANKS, THANKS AND MORE THANKS

❖

I'd like to extend special thanks to the following educators and social workers who lent invaluable assistance in the preparation of this book: Mia Ahntholz, Jennifer Allen, Janet Baker, Shawneece Bradford, Joseph Christie, Michelle Claeys, Jennifer Davis, Kevin Fittinghuff, Dr. Steven Goldstein, Gisella Harvey, Jacqueline Heyward, Jill Horowitz, Sue Kilmer, Suzanne Lynn, Linda McAndris, David Morse, Guy Piotrowsky, Steven Plaut, Lillian Redl, Linda Ritter, Susan Rollins, Cora Sangree, Kate Seid, Stanley Seidman, Chris Shanky, Anne Young, and of course, Bill Clinton, for being the kind of President who engages the interest of children.